W9-BON-016

SandCastle™

Signs of the Seasons

SIGNS OF
Winter

Colleen Dolphin

Consulting Editor,
Diane Craig, M.A./Reading Specialist

A Division of ABDO

ABDO
Publishing Company

visit us at www.abdopublishing.com

Printed in the United States of America, North Mankato, Minnesota
062012
092012

 PRINTED ON RECYCLED PAPER

Editor: Liz Salzmann
Content Developer: Nancy Tuminelly
Cover and Interior Design and Production: Colleen Dolphin, Mighty Media, Inc.
Photo Credits: Shutterstock

Library of Congress Cataloging-in-Publication Data
Dolphin, Colleen, 1979-
  Signs of winter / Colleen Dolphin.
      p. cm. -- (Signs of the seasons)
  ISBN 978-1-61783-395-3 (alk. paper)
  1. Winter--Juvenile literature. 2. Seasons--Juvenile literature. I. Title.
  QB637.8.D65 2013
  508.2--dc23
                            2011052132

SandCastle™ Level: Beginning

SandCastle™ books are created by a team of professional educators, reading specialists, and content developers around five essential components—phonemic awareness, phonics, vocabulary, text comprehension, and fluency—to assist young readers as they develop reading skills and strategies and increase their general knowledge. All books are written, reviewed, and leveled for guided reading, early reading intervention, and Accelerated Reader® programs for use in shared, guided, and independent reading and writing activities to support a balanced approach to literacy instruction. The SandCastle™ series has four levels that correspond to early literacy development. The levels are provided to help teachers and parents select appropriate books for young readers.

Emerging Readers	Beginning Readers	Transitional Readers	Fluent Readers
(no flags)	(1 flag)	(2 flags)	(3 flags)

contents

Seasons 4

Winter 6

Winter Activities 22

Winter Quiz 23

Glossary 24

seasons

There are four seasons during the year. They are called spring, summer, autumn, and winter. The weather, plants, animals, and daylight hours **change** during each season.

winter

spring

summer

autumn

5

winter

During the year, Earth travels around the sun. This brings some parts of Earth closer to the sun. Other parts of Earth get farther from the sun. Winter happens in the parts farthest from the sun.

DID YOU KNOW?

In the winter, there are many clouds in the sky. Instead of raining, it snows. Vanessa and Tom are building a snowman. They start by making a huge snowball.

There is very little daylight in winter. It gets dark out early in the evening.

In winter many trees are bare. Their branches don't have any leaves.

DID YOU KNOW?
Pine and fir trees have **needles**. The needles stay on the trees during winter.

The **temperature** can get very cold during the winter. People need to wear extra clothes to keep warm. James is making a snow **angel**. His coat and snow pants keep him from getting cold.

15

The **temperature** is cold for animals too. Some move to warmer places for the winter. Animals that have a lot of fur stay during the winter. Their fur keeps them warm.

DID YOU KNOW?
An American bison's coat grows extra long and thick in the winter.

DID YOU KNOW?
Winter comes after autumn and before spring.

It is hard for animals to find food in the winter. In autumn, beavers **collect** extra sticks and logs. They keep them in the water near their lodges. They eat the bark during the winter.

Bobby likes to go **sledding** in the winter. What do you do in the winter?

winter activities

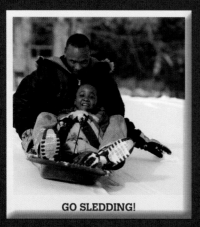

GO SLEDDING!

BUILD A SNOWMAN!

GO SKIING!

BUILD A SNOW FORT!

winter quiz

Read each sentence below. Then decide if it is true or false.

1. The weather **changes** during each season. True or False?

2. There is more daylight in the winter. True or False?

3. Many trees have no leaves in the winter. True or False?

4. It can be very cold in the winter. True or False?

5. Animals can't easily find food in the winter. True or False?

glossary

angel – a spiritual being that looks like a person who has wings.

change – to be altered or become different.

collect – to pick up or gather things from different places.

needle – a thin, pointy leaf on a pine or fir tree.

sled – a wooden or plastic vehicle that you sit on to ride down a snowy hill. Doing this is called *sledding*.

temperature – a measure of how hot or cold something is.